GROUNDS for DISCUSSION

the peaberry chronicles

Michael G. Makemson

Technical Consultant: Brian Dibble

Line and Copy Editing: Rose Ann Clair

Graphic Design: Peaberry Press Vancouver USA

ISBN 9781886638495 (soft cover)

Printed and bound in the USA

10 9 8 7 6 5 4 3 2

Published By:
Peaberry Press Vancouver USA
316 East Seventh Street • Suite 24
Vancouver, WA 98660 (360) 600-3849
E-mail: peaberrypress@comcast.net

Contents

Acknowledgements

In Loving Memory:
Rose Ann Clair
Augusta Makemson

Special Thanks To:
John Burk
Fremont Clair
Brian Dibble
G. Gattis
Wendell & Betty Henry
Rev. Tom McGivney
W. K. Makemson
Brandy Rowell
R. Tamos
Jeanette Thiebert

Introduction

I wrote this book to share my passion of coffee with you. Over the years I have told many stories about my life. Looking back, there was a common thread in many of them—coffee. The *Peaberry Chronicles* are those personal stories. Some may directly involve coffee. While others are simply stories to be enjoyed as you sip your favorite beverage. The book also takes you on a journey of coffee history, harvesting, roasting and brewing. And of course, there are some of my favorite time-tested recipes that would satisfy even the most discriminating of palates.

Years ago, my family used to pile into the car for a Sunday drive—no agenda. Today, our fast paced world of smart phones and tablets leaves little room for such care free indulgences. It is my hope that we can slow down and enjoy the moment for the moment. The Italian expression *"dolce far niente"* (sweet idleness) aptly describes this. I invite you to pour your favorite beverage, sit back, and enjoy the book.

Sis, myself and our doberman, Buttons

"I have measured out my life with coffee spoons."

.... *T. S. Eliot (1888-1965)*

My first taste of coffee came as a kid growing up in rural Indiana in the 1950s. We lived in a peaceful, cozy community of cottages nestled between Little and Big Chapman Lakes. There was the summer crowd of course but many of the houses were occupied by resident dwellers like ourselves. Winters were always fun for us kids. It seemed like we always got tons of fresh snow, which blanketed the entire area. Bundled up with mittens clipped to our sleeves, my sister and I would play for hours on end in the snow. We stayed outside almost to the point of exhaustion and then drug ourselves into the house where Mom would have hot cocoa waiting for us. When company came over, she would break out the percolator and put on a pot of coffee. I always headed to the kitchen to watch her get the Mirro-Matic® ready. Her brand of coffee was Hills Bros®. It came in cans that were called key-wind tins. As Mom turned the key and broke the seal, there would be a very distinctive hissing sound. The unmistakable aroma of freshly ground coffee, once

Mirro-Matic® coffee maker like the one featured on many episodes of "I Love Lucy"

held captive, was now released in all of its glory, filling the room with an intoxicating aroma. Next came the water. Placing a finger over the stem, she carefully added the ground coffee—leveling off at the 4, 6, 8, or 10-cup markings etched on the inside of the filter basket. The amounts were not arbitrary but set by the Pan American Coffee Bureau, then considered to be the gold standard of coffee brewing. You could always be assured of a good cup of coffee when you saw the distinctive *Gold Cup Award* hanging on a restaurant wall. With the lid secured and the pot plugged in, the stage was set for action. Water began spurting up into the glass knob on top of the lid, turning darker and darker as the brewing cycle came to an end. Watching it, smelling the aroma, and listening to the rhythm was absolutely mesmerizing. The adults would get *café au lait*. For the kids it would be milk with a little bit of coffee— just enough to feel grown up.

Entertaining back in the 1950s certainly meant breaking out the hospitality snack plates made by Federal Glass®. Mom had the clear ones with a wheat pattern molded into the bottom. She filled the plates with little sandwiches, mints, and sometimes store-bought butter cookies. Since home baking was so commonplace, it was a real treat to get

Hospitality snack plate
and Mother's® butter cookies

"Good to the last drop."

....President Theodore Roosevelt in describing
Maxwell House® Coffee (1907)

Mother's® butter cookies from the local IGA. We were dunkers! The challenge was seeing how much of the cookie actually made it into our mouths without breaking apart and sinking to the bottom of the cup. My neighbors, Butch and Molly always had a stash of her signature buttermilk sugar cookies tucked away for me. The red Currier and Ives tin filled with the cookies was located in the bottom cupboard—easy reach for a little guy. These tasty morsels soaked up the milk or coffee like little sponges. When I got the urge all I had to do was head down to their cottage and grab a few. Molly also kept small bottles of Coke® for me in the fridge—remember those? Roaming the neighborhood would often draw the attention of my mother, and land me in the proverbial dog house—confined to the yard. A long utility pole anchored in the ground marked the out of bounds. Even at the tender age of five I would tempt fate by sitting on the pole and firmly planting my little feet just on the other side. Butch would often come over and sit down next to me, lending a sympathetic ear to my tales of woe. It seemed like an eternity. However, it wasn't long until the restriction was lifted and I was free to explore the neighborhood once again—giving me plenty of opportunity to get into more mischief.

Hills Bros.® key wind tin - 1945

Hills Bros.® branded coffee scoop

"For Any Method of Coffee - Making"

These instructions were printed on the back panel of a vintage Hills Bros.® tin

Measure Carefully:
2 <u>level</u> tablespoons of coffee to each cup of water. Vary water slightly for exact strength desired. Consistent timing is important. Keep coffee-maker clean.

Coffeepot:
Bring coffee and water <u>just</u> to boiling point. Remove from heat. Stir well. Add small amount of cold water and let stand 5 minutes to settle grounds.

Steeping:
Pour boiling water on coffee. Stir well. Stir again in 5 minutes. Steep 5 to 10 minutes more. Keep hot but do not boil.

Percolator:
"Perk" gently 7 to 10 minutes after pumping starts.

Vacuum Method:
Put upper bowl on <u>after</u> water boils. Stir mixture well in upper bowl. Control heat to keep water and coffee in contact 5 to 7 minutes.

Drip Method:
Use fresh, briskly boiling water. If less than 2/3 capacity is made, water may drip too fast, giving weak brew. When dripping is completed, remove upper section. Stir, brew and serve.

Kaldi and the dancing goats

History

Coffee is thought to have originated in Ethiopia. From there comes one of the more popular legends surrounding it—Kaldi and the goats. Almost any coffee book that you pick up includes such stories. Reluctant to follow that well worn path myself, two Ethiopian college students from a local university convinced me otherwise. I asked them if they were familiar with the legend and they replied, "Of course, in Ethiopia it has been passed down for centuries as a children's bedtime story. You must include it in your book, it's a piece of coffee history."

The legend begins with Kaldi, an Abyssinian goatherder trying to solve the mystery of why his goats never slept—constantly frolicking and munching on red berries from surrounding shrubs. A monk from a neighboring monastery investigated and came to the conclusion that the berries (actually ripe coffee cherries loaded with caffeine) were the source of the goats' insomnia—solving the mystery. Supposedly, the resourceful monks concocted beverages from the cherries—enhancing their attentiveness during evening prayers.

Before the advent of roasting, green beans were combined with animal fat to make a type of trail food. Coffee cherries were boiled to make

"Coffee should be black
as hell, strong as death,
and sweet as love."

....Turkish proverb

teas. Wines were made by allowing a mixture of pulp and skins to ferment. Interestingly, the Arabic word for coffee, *qahwah*, also refers to wine.

Cultivation of coffee plants began around 600 A.D. By the sixteenth century beans were being roasted and ground. The grounds were steeped or infused in hot water resulting in a liquid so potent that it was thought to have therapeutic properties—reserved for the medical practitioners of the day. The Arabs who were very protective of their coffee trade put security measures in place to prevent the exportation of fertile plants and beans. Despite this, the Dutch were able to break through the security and obtain seedlings. As a special gift for King Louis XIV, they presented him with a few of the plants which he nurtured in the Jardin des Plantes in Paris. Story has it that French Naval officer, Gabriel Mathieau de Clieu absconded with one of the plants, taking it back to his duty station in French Martinique. The ocean voyage for both he and plant was treacherous. Due to his vigilance (sharing his own water ration with it) the plant survived. His hunch that coffee plants would thrive in the climate of Martinque was correct and would eventually lead

Even in that land of good living - - - it was a place of wonders

Everybody was eager to see it—the kitchen of this most famous hotel of the Old South. Was it not here that the food was produced which was celebrated throughout all Dixie?

"A majestic edifice," declared the dignified newspapers of the day, now yellow with age, in summing up the glories of the old Maxwell House in Nashville. But the beaux and belles who danced at the courtly balls gave their chief praise, not to its marbles and mirrors, but—to the good things to eat and drink that came out of the kitchen!

Year after year, the noted folk of the South, gathering for the great balls and banquets at the old Maxwell House, revelled in its food and its coffee. Year after year they came to visit Antoine himself in his kitchen. And many were the distinguished visitors to that land of good living who were taken to see that place of wonders.

What a sight it was to cheer the inner man! Here was the "immense roasting jack" where haunches of venison were browned to a turn. Here was the carving room and here the enormous ovens where wild turkey and prairie grouse, pompano and terrapin, were conjured into such dishes as history is made of.

But always Antoine and his guests stopped longest before the ruddy urn from which came the coffee which was to win the Maxwell House the greatest fame of all.

The news of it spread rapidly
It was a special blend of coffee that was

"Good to the last drop"

served at the Maxwell House, full-flavored and richly mellow like no other kind. More than anything else, the guests of this fine old hotel praised its coffee and spread its fame when they returned home. Soon this blend was known and used in every southern state.

Today, still blended and roasted by the same firm of coffee merchants who perfected it years ago down in Nashville, Maxwell House Coffee is on sale in sealed tins throughout the United States. It is the first choice of a long list of the nation's greatest cities. It is pleasing more people than any other coffee ever offered for sale.

What rare pleasure you can give your family tomorrow when they first taste Maxwell House Coffee! They can have the same flavor and wonderful aroma that roused the enthusiasm of guests at the old Maxwell House years ago. Your grocer has the famous blue tins.

Cheek-Neal Coffee Company, Nashville, Houston, Jacksonville, Richmond, New York, Los Angeles.

MAXWELL HOUSE COFFEE *
TODAY — *America's largest selling high grade coffee*

November 1926 Good Housekeeping

Maxwell House® Coffee ad
"Good Housekeeping" - Nov. 1926

to the propagation and establishment of plantations in the West Indies.

Another influential and colorful character in coffee history was Francisco de Melho Palheta. As an arbitrator and surveyor, he was called upon to settle a territorial dispute between the coffee producing colonies of Dutch and French Guiana. In the process of resolving the conflict he found himself in a brief but intimate relationship with the French governor's wife. She was so enamored with him that on his departure a bouquet of flowers concealing a fertile coffee plant was given to him as a parting gift. He took the seedling back to Brazil and saw to its growth and development. That solitary plant was the start of what is now an enormous coffee empire.

Coffee's popularity would soon spill over into various parts of the world. It had an intoxicating appeal to those who consumed it, so much so that it was viewed by some as the work of Satan. Pope Clement VIII (1592 to 1605, n. Ippolito Aldo Brandini) who enjoyed coffee himself, intervened on its behalf saying, "Why this Satan's drink is so delicious that it would be a pity to let the infidels have exclusive use of it. We shall fool Satan by baptizing it, and making it a truly Christian beverage" (William H. Ukers, *All About Coffee* - 1935).

"Nescafe no es cafe."
(Instant coffee is not
coffee.)

....*Mexican Saying*

By the late 1600s coffeehouses would begin to emerge. They often drew the attention of religious and political leaders who considered them hotbeds of intellectual discontent. Once considered a central meeting place to disseminate news and information, the coffee house would decline somewhat in popularity, due in part to the availability and distribution of newspapers. Nevertheless, many coffeehouses have survived and continue to flourish across Europe even to this day.

Up to this point, coffee had been roasted and boiled in water producing a liquid called a decoction. Infusion or steeping would replace it as a preferred method of extraction without boiling—reducing bitterness and capturing more flavor. A variety of French pots came on the scene. One used a cloth bag to contain the ground coffee. Extraction took place as the water was poured over the bag with the liquid dripping into the bottom container—all by a process of gravity. Vacuum pots would go a step further by using not only gravity but a partial vacuum to *pull* the water through the grounds. Their fragility (being made of glass and easily broken) did not diminish the fascination of watching the brewing process in action.

Caffeine

There are over a 1000 chemical components making up the flavor and aroma of coffee— caffeine being one of them. A bitter and odorless white powder, caffeine is practically synonymous with the word coffee— promoting frequent trips to the bathroom, aiding digestion, and enhancing concentration and alertness. *Arabicas* naturally contain less caffeine than *robustas*, about half as much.

Chemical structure of caffeine - trimethylxanthine

The next major development in brewing technology would come from Italian innovators like Luigi Bezzera (1901). He developed a machine which utilized trapped steam pressure to *push* the water through the grounds into brewing groups and individual cups, much like espresso machines of today. Others like Desiderio Pavoni and Pier Teresio Arduino followed suit. But trapped steam had its limitations—1½ atmospheres of pressure compared to machines of today at 9 or more. Early in the 1940s, Achille Gaggia would find a way of breaking the '1½ atmosphere barrier' by inventing a machine with a spring-lever piston, increasing the pressure by six to nine times. The piston was charged by pulling down and then releasing a handle. Baristas still use the term, *pulling a shot* to describe that individual action of brewing.

Of course, machines today have electrically driven pumps and temperatures controlled by micro computers. Espresso is so much a part of our daily lives that we tend to forget its humble beginnings. Pour overs, specialty espresso beverages, Keurig® and Nespresso® machines dominate our coffee drinking culture. Percolators are rarely used any more. However, there has been a resurgence of the old brewing devices such as the French Press and vacuum brewer.

Monarch® coffee jar with lion head logo

Something A Jar

Indiana schools never shut down until there was at least a foot and a half of snow on the ground. We would gather around the Zenith® radio in the kitchen, listening intently for school closures on WRSW. When Pierceton was mentioned, I knew the day was mine. Even so, there were the daily chores. First priority was feeding Fuzzy, my cat. He would be patiently waiting on the porch step for a bowl of warm milk. Then it was down to the basement to stoke the fire and take out the ashes. Out of the corner of my eye I happened to notice something on the ledge near the furnace. Underneath cobwebs, dust, and years of accumulated soot was a glass jar. I carefully wiped off the label, revealing an image of a lion. It read 'Monarch Coffee - Reid, Murdoch & Co., Net Weight: 1 Pound.' Handwritten in pencil in the upper right corner was the price—39 cents, Wow!

Established in 1853, Reid, Murdoch & Co. was a packer and distributor of spices and food products based out of Chicago. There were many processing plants scattered across the country, including one in Pierceton. My grandmother would often tell us stories about working on the line, bottling ketch-up. Apart from coffee, they also canned sweet corn, peas, yellow cling peaches and red raspberries, just to name a few.

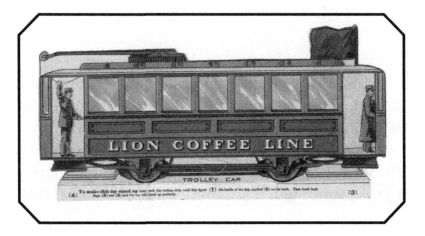

Lion Coffee® produced hundreds of seasonal greeting cards and childrens' toys packed inside with their coffee.

Back panel of childrens' paper toy.
Tabs were bent back so it would stand up.

Unfortunately, between graduate school and many moves, I lost track of that old jar. As luck would have it another would come my way. It was taller and shaped a little differently but had all of the hallmarks of a genuine Monarch complete with the 'Lion Head' logo (one of the oldest trade marks in the U.S.). The lid, which was original to the piece, showed usual signs of wear. Yet, it still retained its colorful and vivid graphics. This jar would certainly be a welcomed addition to my collection.

After moving to Oregon, I was eager to get on a bike once again. Don't envision me as an off-road kind of guy. Yes, I had a mountain bike, affectionately known as *The Tunturi® Stead*, but sought out the smooth, paved roads, not trails. One Sunday morning I pedaled to Lafayette—a little over 5 miles from McMinnville. The weather was picture perfect—bright and sunny, cattle grazing in the fields, and Mt. Hood in the background. Nestled in the middle of wine country, Lafayette was home to an old schoolhouse that had been converted into an antique mall. It had three floors filled to brim with treasures of days gone by. I headed up to the second floor to a space jammed full of coffee pots, pans and kitchen gadgets. Several mason jars were lined up

Golden West® coffee jar -
Closset & Devers

on the window sill, silhouetted by the morning sun. Right in the middle was a square, pale blue jar with a tin lid. Molded into the glass were the words, 'Golden West Vacuum Packed Coffee, Closset and Devers, Portland, Ore.' I had to have it! It wasn't just another coffee jar but one that was from this part of the Pacific Northwest. Closset and Devers (est. 1883) was a purveyor of coffee, tea, spices, and baking powder. According to Polk's Portland City Directory of 1931, they were located at the corner of Northwest Fifteenth Ave. and Pettygrove Street. In the days of switchboards and operators, you could call them up by saying, "Central, give me Broadway 0314." One of the first to vacuum-pack coffee, Closset and Devers would establish Golden West® as one of their signature brands. Cans or jars bearing that logo are much sought after by collectors today.

I was still looking for an antique coffee grinder and in particular a side grinder—called as such because it was designed to be mounted on the side of a cabinet or table. And there it was, right in front of me, an Increase Wilson® side grinder (Mfg. in New London Connecticut, circa 1850). Typically, these grinders were mounted on a small piece of wood with three pre-drilled holes. Turning it over I recognized a handwritten name that had been penciled

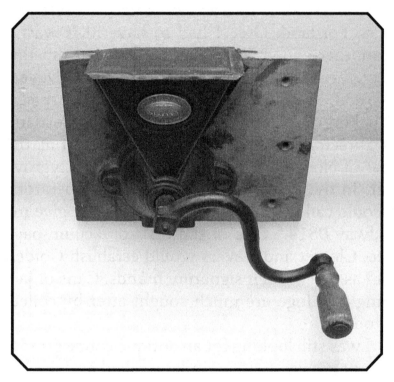

Increase Wilson side grinder - 1850s

in—'Mrs. Lindstrum.' Incredibly it was the same grinder that I had found from the year before—still in the same location with the same price. Not wanting to risk losing it, I plucked it from the wall and headed straight down to the checkout counter.

Yes, there were many more unexplored rooms. But they would just have to wait for the next Sunday bike ride.

Increase Wilson® name plate

Coffee

family: *Rubiaceae*
genus: *Coffea*
species: over 60

World Market
of Coffee

Arabica (Grown at higher elevations) — 75%
Robusta (Grown at lower elevations) — 25%

Top Five Coffee
Producing Countries

Brazil
Vietnam
Colombia
Indonesia
Ethiopia

Harvesting

By all appearances the coffee plant looks like a tree. Actually, it is an evergreen shrub, growing to cultivated heights of 8 to 15 feet. Over 60 species have been identified, but only two are marketed on a wide scale—*coffea arabica* and *robusta*. The sweet, jasmine-scented, white blossoms signal the oncoming cherries, which turn from green to yellow and then crimson when ripe. A cherry usually contains two seeds (beans). When only one seed develops, it takes on an oval or round shape—much like that of a pea. Hence the name, peaberry. Coffee plants begin producing marketable quantities of beans in 3 to 5 years and will continue to do so for 15 or more years. Arabicas ripen in 6 to 8 months, whereas robustas can take up to 11 months. Major brands of coffee, quite commonly, contain blends of arabicas and robustas.

Depending on the amount of rainfall, harvesting sometimes requires more than one visit to the plant during a season. A branch may contain blossoms, ripe, and unripe cherries simultaneously. Unripe cherries will not continue to ripen if picked prematurely, and overripe cherries are not usable, at least from a marketing standpoint. Hand picking, where only the ripe cherries are selected, remains

In the warehouse

the preferred method of harvesting. However, it is the most expensive. On the average, a worker can pick about 200 lbs. of cherries per day (about 40 lbs. of green beans). Filled bags of beans weigh between 100 to 152 lbs. Once the cherries have been harvested they are processed rather quickly to extract the beans. Arabicas are usually processed by the wet method where the cherries are run through a machine which removes the pulp, leaving behind the parchment skins (nature's protective shell). Any remaining mucilage is removed by fermentation and washing. Then, over the course of about two weeks, the beans are dried—preserving the much sought-after quality and the recognizable bluish-green color. Hulling of the parchment and polishing of the beans removes any residual silver skins that may have been left behind. After the beans are sorted and graded, they are stored in warehouses awaiting export.

Julian Public Library - 1971
Originally, Santa Ysabel School at Witch Creek - 1880
Currently, home of the Julian Historical Society

World's Greatest Coffee

Three Hospital Corpsman from Camp Pend-leton would embark on a weekend camping trip —their destination, the Anza-Borrego Desert State Park. Located about 40 miles east of Escondido, it was one of California's largest state park. But how could a place by day be so hot and yet bone-chillingly cold at night—after all it was a desert? We had planned for weeks and even made pounds of beef jerky—using our old-style gas oven that doubled as a dehydrator. The base PX outfitted us with all kinds of camping gear—sleeping bags, tents, lanterns, back packs, stove, and even long underwear. With hiking boots already on board, all I needed was a good reliable knife. A Gerber® flayer would do the trick—with its unique, teardrop-shaped blade, molded leather sheath, and sharpening steel. Friends suggested stocking up on firewood. Because as they said, "It tends to get a little chilly out there." Our adventure had all of the trappings of a photo shoot for Coleman®. Gear in tow, we set out for the desert—stopping along the way to draw some water from a local spring. We drove into the wee hours of the morning and actually slept in the car in front of a Chevron® in Julian. This would guarantee our place in line for gas rationing the next morning.

Anza-Borrego landscape

Roger (L) & Glen preparing food

After a great breakfast of ham, eggs, hash browns, and plenty of coffee, we headed out. Entering the Anza-Borrego Desert State Park, we drove for what seemed like miles and then made our turn onto a desert wash. The odometer rolled over, 'one, two, three,' coming to rest on the five mile mark. Keep in mind that we weren't riding in a SUV but rather my brand new 1971 Cutlass Supreme. At any moment I expected the tires to sink in the sand up to the axles. Instead, the wash supported the car and acted like a regular, paved road. Glancing out of the windows, we all chanted in perfect unison, "This is the place!" We were miles from anywhere. It was so quiet that you could practically hear your heart beating. The sky was a breathtaking robin-egg blue. More accustomed to a smoldering firing range on a military base, we sampled the clean air as if it were a fine wine—a Châteauneuf-du-Pape. We worked up enormous appetites setting up the base camp. It was no easy task! The wind had picked up, making it especially difficult to anchor the tent stakes in the sand. For an added measure of security, we piled heavy rocks on top of the stakes. Reasonably satisfied that our tents would not collapse through the night, we celebrated our victory by throwing on some T-bones, sitting around the camp fire, and tell-

"I can still taste those steaks."

"Coffee has two virtues: it's wet and warm."

....Dutch saying

ing stories and jokes into the wee hours of the morning. Finally, it was time to turn in. Glen chose to brave the elements in his sleeping bag outside. Roger and I opted for the comfort of our tents.

However, in just a few short hours, I would be abruptly awakened from a sound sleep by intense itching and burning. Peeling off the long johns, huge welts could be seen covering most of my legs. Was I being attacked by insects or some kind of little critters? The label on the waist band would tell it all—WOOL! I was allergic to wool! I knew the shirt tops were made of cotton but never thought for a moment that the long johns would be made of wool. I quickly peeled them off, took some Benadryl® from the first-aid kit and snuggled back into the warmth of my mountain down sleeping bag.

The next morning Roger and I woke to an amazing sight. Glen was still sound asleep outside. His moist breath and the frigid night air had transformed his mustache into an ice sculpture. Why in the world didn't I get a snapshot of that? I stoked the fire and started the coffee—using the spring water that we collected earlier. The coffee pot was not much to look at—a Saturday flea market special with a wobbly handle. The coffee was not JBM (Jamaica

At the summit - the arrowhead lays just inches below my feet.

Arrowhead found at Anza-Borrego

Blue Mountain®). Instead, it was MJB® right out of the can. They say that hot dogs always taste better at the ballpark and camp coffee was no exception. We were so cold and shivering that it would be deemed 'The World's Greatest Coffee.' After a few warming cups, along with bacon and eggs, we were ready for a day of exploration.

The 2500 ft. climb to the top of the mountain was a work out, even for us Navy guys. Reaching the summit, I surveyed the breathtaking landscape and sat down on a boulder to rest a bit. And there between my feet was of all things, an arrowhead! The brochure said that this area was known for its 'rich archaeological history.' What were the odds that **we** would discover an artifact in such a casual way? After all, we weren't looking or digging for it. It was just lying there on the surface.

Glen, Roger, and I stayed for two more nights, climbing more hills, eating like kings, and sharing stories. Our camping trip would soon be coming to an end but the memories would last a lifetime.

Pulling the roast

Roasting Stages

*By the end of roasting, temperatures
can reach as high as 450°.*

*Wheat or Green to Yellow Roast
(5 to 7 min.)*
Yellow-orange in color,
beans lose moisture

Cinnamon Roast
'First Pop,' beans start to unfold,
increase in size,
acidity is very high

City Roast (10 to 11 min.)
'American Roast,' light brown in color,
acidity is good

Full City Roast (12 to 14 min.)
Peak of flavor, brown, balance of
body and acidity maintained

Dark Roast (14 min. and beyond)
Tasting the roast (eg. smoky),

Tasting Criteria

Aroma
...the fragrance of the coffee,
eg. during a cupping when
the crust is broken

Body
...the perceptive weight of the
coffee on the palate

Acidity
...the liveliness or briskness
of the coffee, not to be
confused with pH acidity

Flavor
...the complexity, richness
and balance, eg. winey, exotic,
wild, earthy, tangy, mild,
sweet, soft, spicy

Nine Great Coffees Grouped By Body

Mild
Kona
Brazilian
Mexican Altura

Medium
Kenya AA
Colombian
Guatemala Antigua

Heavy
Ethiopian Harrar
Sulawesi
Sumatra

The 'Coffee Break' is still very much a part
of the American culture.

Coffee, "The favorite drink of the civilised world."

.... *Thomas Jefferson*

On December 16, 1773, colonial rebels protested against England and her time-honored and highly taxed beverage of more than 200 years. They dumped hundreds of pounds of tea into Boston Harbor. Coffee was then declared the patriot's drink—soon to be solidified as America's drink.

Some innovative Civil War muskets actually had built-in grinders. Soldiers were issued a ration of whole beans which could be ground to brew coffee at the campsite. It became a familiar part of a G.I.'s life during World War II—taking on the nickname of 'Cuppa-Joe.'

The day begins for many Americans with the ritual cup of coffee. Some are awakened by the aroma from automatic coffee makers. Others use French Presses, Neapolitan flip pots, percolators, vacuum pots, and espresso makers. Some catch a cup on the way to work at their favorite cafés or drive throughs. Others enjoy a cup with friends, at home, or reading the morning newspaper.

Jamaica Blue Mountain® coffee barrel

Keeping It Fresh

to insure the most flavorful cup of coffee

There are varied opinions on the storage of coffee beans but here are a few simple measures that you can take to maintain freshness.

1. Buy only the amount of whole bean coffee that you will use in the course of about two weeks.

2. Store in an air-tight, opaque container at room temperature, out of direct sunlight. Coffee is vulnerable to air, heat, light, and moisture—being highly absorbable (hydroscopic).

3. Refrigerating or freezing the beans is not recommended. If you do, make sure that you use containers that are completely air-tight.

4. Grind just before brewing.

Most of us can remember...Eight O'Clock®
bean coffee ground to order.

Coffee tin - 1950s

Grinding and Grinders

Grinding beans at the time of brewing is at the heart of good coffee.

Blade grinders fracture the beans as the blades whirl around—much like a blender or food processor. It is difficult to maintain consistency, but it gets the job done.

Burr grinders, on the other hand, have grinding wheels which allow more precise adjustment of the size of the grind. **I highly recommend this type of grinder and one that is capable of producing the consistency needed to brew espresso as well.**

Pick a model that has replaceable parts and easily removable blade assemblies for cleaning. Granted, they cost more ($200 plus), but are well worth the investment.

Cafetiere or French Press

Take the Plunge

Dating back to the turn of the century, the French Press remains my favorite vessel in which to brew coffee. Also, known as the press pot or *cafetiere*, it produces an intense, flavorful brew with full body. I first encountered such a pot in a quaint, little café on the north side of Milwaukee. Each person had their own individual pot—so personal, so interactive, so visual. Coarsely ground, the coffee is allowed to steep. As you plunge, the result is a silky, creamy layer that floats on top. Because the oils and fine sediment are not filtered off, you retain all of the great flavor in your cup.

The simple elegance of the French Press allows you to enjoy a cup of coffee like no other brewing method.

Tips on Brewing
consistency is the key

1. Water should be fresh and good tasting. Use filtered or bottled water if necessary. Heat the water to just off the boil.

2. Grind size should match the type of pot that you are using. Preferably grind whole beans at the time of brewing.

3. Proportion of coffee and water are critical. Use 1 approved CBC (Coffee Brewing Council) level scoop: 2 tbsp. for each 6 oz. of water.

One of the more popular methods of brewing today is the **pour over**. It's a new take on the filter drip process invented years ago. Coffee and water are precisely weighed in a ratio of 1:15 (1 gram of coffee for 15 grams of water). Timing each segment carefully, water is poured over in a way that continually replenishes the grounds, allowing for optimal extraction and flavor.

Making Coffee in the French Press

1. Clean all parts of the press using hot water and a mild detergent.

2. Charge the press and the cups by pouring hot water into them—discard.

4. Add coarsely ground coffee: one coffee measure (2 tbsp.) for each 6 oz. of water.

5. Pour half of the water (just off the boil) over the the grounds. The grounds will puff up—creating the 'bloom effect.' **Wait one minute.** Break the crust with a spoon allowing the gas to escape.

6. Gently add the remaining water in a swirling motion and place the wire mesh plunger on top of the grounds—allowing the lid to slide down and cover the top. **Wait three minutes.**

7. Press down on the plunger evenly and slowly.

8. Pour out immediately. Allowing the coffee to remain in the press will result in over extraction.

"If this is coffee, then please bring me some tea. But if this is tea, please bring me some coffee."

.... *Abraham Lincoln (1809-1865)*

Handle of a teaspoon - The Drake, Chicago

Dolce Far Niente
sweet idleness

From My Journal

Saturday, Nov. 24, 1990
The Drake Hotel, Chicago

Very cold. Hasn't snowed as of yet.
Semester is over. Finals are done. What a
relief! Ryan and I arrive at the The Drake.
Too early for Afternoon Tea at the Palm
Court. We sipped our coffee on the nearby
terrace. Waiter poured from an elegant silver
pot. Gold-rimmed china cups, starched linens.
 Fascinating, just watching the people.
A gentleman seated at the next table was
impeccably dressed—three piece vested suit,
French cuffs, bow tie, bone-rimmed glasses
and an immaculately trimmed beard. Reminded
me of Robert Fulghum, the author—especially
the tie. You never know, maybe it was he!
 We stayed for lunch at the Cape Cod
Room. Marilyn Monroe and Joe DiMaggio carved
their initials into the top of the bar. Ryan
suggested the New England Clam Chowder.
Great choice!

"How do you like your eggs?" "In coffee," you say.

Egg Coffee

The Christmas season in particular ushers in fond memories of family and friends getting together to share great food and drink. What vividly comes to mind is the amazing coffee that a family friend used to make as we gathered for holiday dinners. A wonderful aroma greeted us at Anna's front door. Making my way back to the kitchen I soon discovered the source—coffee simmering in a blue and white speckled pot on the back burner. The ladies were sitting around the kitchen table, chatting back and forth, sharing their version of how to make the coffee—"Bring the water to a boil, add an egg, a pinch of salt..." The conversation piqued my curiosity but didn't have a great deal of meaning for me at the time—I was only 11 or 12. Many years later, on a Sunday walk in a shopping mall, I spied a unique demitasse (small cup for espresso) in the window of a shop, specializing in Italian ceramics. Sharing my interest in coffee prompted the clerk to describe what she called her Grandma Fidelia's 'egg coffee.' The similarities were too coincidental. Could this be the same kind of coffee that the ladies were talking about at those family dinners? There was only one way to find out and that was to make

Egg Coffee

• Use regular grind coffee: 2 tablespoons for each 6 oz. of water.

• Pinch of salt

• 1 egg

1. Combine ground coffee, salt, and egg (well beaten) in a bowl. Mixture should resemble a paste. Optional: May add crumbled egg shell to the mix.

2. Heat water to just off the boil.

3. Add coffee mixture and stir.

4. Simmer for five minutes. Grounds will clump together, resembling a big cork.

5. Decant using a ladle.

it myself. Following her directions to the letter, I was pleasantly surprised as the aroma wafted through my entire apartment—permeating every nook and cranny. The end result was a clear, full-bodied brew with a mild, yet robust taste. One very interesting thing about egg coffee is that it can be refrigerated and reheated while maintaining much of its original flavor. Egg coffee has always been a customary part of Scandanavian church gatherings, family dinners, and wakes. It's always fun to make during the holidays as kids look on. They will be utterly fascinated at how an 'egg' is used in making this wonderful coffee.

Thanks to Grandma Fidelia, the mystery has been solved.

Lou Mitchell's - "serving the world's finest coffee"
Jackson Blvd. (Historic U. S. Route 66) - Chicago

Lou Mitchell's - The great people that serve your food

Double-Yolked Eggs, Coffee and Milk Duds®

The weekend in Chicago was a birthday gift from my friend, Todd. He had it all planned out. We would stay at a fine hotel, have a nice dinner, take in the symphony and then have breakfast the following morning at a famous diner.

Checking in at the Palmer House seemed to take longer than usual—but after all it was Friday evening. As I sat there, soaking in the grandeur of the magnificent lobby, I curiously watched as people passed by—wondering who they were, where they were from and what their plans for the evening would be. Todd returned with kind of a grin on his face, and said, "We're all set." After a few minutes we arrived at our room. Opening the door, he asked, "Well, do you like it?" I just stood there, dumbfounded. This was no ordinary room. It was a suite—big screen TV's, a sitting room, two bedrooms, bar, and a refrigerator chock-full of liver pâtés, caviar, and champagne. Apparently there was a reservation mix-up and this was the only room left.

Lou Mitchell's -
We sat in the middle. All the booths were taken.
It had the feeling of an old-fashioned diner.

"Coffee is not my cup of tea."

....Samuel Goldwyn

We were then off to the symphony. It was absolutely breathtaking under the direction of Sir George Solti—Bach with a full chorus. Not wanting to call it a night quite yet, we poured some nightcaps, lounged around the suite and reminisced about the evening. The next morning would bring subzero temperatures as we waited in line to get into Lou Mitchell's, one of Chicago's iconic breakfast places. They didn't call it 'the windy city' for nothing—as frigid air from Lake Michigan swept over us on Jackson Street. Waiting outside did have its rewards. From a wicker basket came Milk Duds (for the ladies & kids) or doughnut holes (for the gents)—a tradition started by Lou himself. Once inside, Todd and I sat across from each other in cafeteria style. First came the coffee, freshly ground and brewed. Lou Mitchell's is all about freshness. Even the orange and grapefruit juices are freshly squeezed. I had a ham and cheese, double-yolked omelette, and hash browns—served in its individual skillet. Scrumptious! Todd had the Belgium waffles which looked pretty darn good. Finishing it off, an orange wedge and prune to balance out the gastronomical delight.

As we departed, I glanced up at the billboard which read, "*Selected Number 1 Breakfast and Lunch Restaurant in America.*" I couldn't have agreed more. What a fitting end to a memorable weekend.

The Academy bell tower - Vancouver, WA

A Higher Calling
from the seminary

Back in the 1980s I was called, or thought so at least, to the Roman Catholic priesthood. Being relatively new to the faith, and a convert at that, I had no idea what was in store for me. Over the course of six years, my studies would take me to three distinctively different seminaries scattered around the country. The first was a medieval looking, monastic place right out of a Harry Potter movie. The second was one of the oldest and most conservative seminaries in the country. The third and final school was designed for delayed vocations and older guys like myself.

The second school is where my story unfolds. Among other things, this seminary had a very strict dress code. When attending class you were expected to wear a black clerical shirt with a white tab collar (A.K.A. the *Roomey Toomey*), black slacks, black blazer and black shoes. After evening prayers, we all gathered for dinner in a separate dining room at the college—a quarter of a mile away.

First year theologians were all designated to serve at various liturgical functions. As 'luck' would have it, using the word loosely, I was chosen to assist the priest at Benediction. The attire for this would be a black cassock (long robe) and surplice

"The morning cup of coffee has an exhilaration about it which the cheering influence of the afternoon or evening cup of tea cannot be expected to reproduce."

....Oliver Wendell Holmes, Sr. (1809-1894)

(white tunic) over it. The cassock was a gift from a vested priest who had worn it years earlier at his college seminary. It was indeed an honor to carry on the tradition. The surplice was from Gammarelli's (outfitters to the Pope) of Rome. Made from Irish linen with a hand embroidered cross on the front and a square yoke collar, it was referred to as the *Papal Vaticani* (used at the Vatican)—much sought after by my fellow seminarians. I felt like a model, on the runway, showing off the latest in liturgical fashion. Leading the way, I headed down the isle swinging the thurible (containing the hot incense). Everything was going smoothly. The priest incensed the altar, handed the thurible back to me, and we both knelt. He began to pray, "Come Lord Jesus" followed by a long pause and then another "Come Lord Jesus" and then another pause. At that very moment I felt an intense burning sensation on my right leg. Looking down, I discovered that the thurible had burned through my cassock, scorching my trousers. The deafening quietude of the chapel was broken as I blurted out the words, "Oh my God!" Quickly, I patted the area to extinguish any additional smoldering. Nothing was ever said about the incident until a couple of weeks later when another

My copy of
Uker's, "All About Coffee" finally arrives.
The blueberry bran muffin—one of my favorites.

seminarian approached me. He said, "I thought you were having some kind of a spiritual awakening." I almost felt obligated to confess that it was just a reactionary response to nearly going up in flames. However, if he thought it was an awakening of sorts—so be it.

I always felt a little awkward wearing the clerical shirts—given my newness to the faith. Eventually, the feeling would wear off, but it still didn't diminish the fact that we all looked like priests—and were not ordained. And people treated us differently when we wore the clerical shirts.

This came into play when a college student literally ran into me on my way to dinner one evening. Almost knocking us both to the ground, she uttered a few *expletives* and glanced up, noticing my clerical shirt. I'll never forget the look on her face. Probably in her mind, she had just sworn a blue streak in the presence of a priest, or even worse, one of her professors. I was older and certainly looked the part. All that I could think of saying to her at that point was "You have a good evening, now." She must have felt that some type of repercussion would take place. Little did she know that I posed no threat at all. I was just another seminarian on my way to dinner.

"Coffee smells like freshly ground heaven."

....*Jessi Lane Adams*

Apart from our academic training, we were expected to do apostolic or volunteer work in the community. This varied from distributing Holy Communion to just visitations—similar to Catholic social work. Interestingly, the geographic area surrounding the seminary was very compelling. It was the 1980s and yet people were living in abject poverty—dirt floors and no indoor plumbing. I was absolutely shocked. How could this be in this day and age? Seminarians often complained about sharing rooms, the lack of private bathrooms and showers. After making a few community visits like this, we had no room to complain. My counterpart, John and I, were paired up for the semester. He was refreshingly funny and spoke with a pronounced New Jersey accent. We made quite the pair going out on pastoral visits. One of our first visits took us up a narrow, winding lane where we noticed a man standing next to an old wooden fence, waving us over. We introduced ourselves. His name was Bert and he had been expecting us. A Belgian draft horse was grazing in the nearby pasture. "Would you like to give Jane a carrot?" he asked. Knowing my past luck with horses (kicking and biting), I was somewhat reluctant but agreed. He called her name. Here she came, at a full gallop, stopping just short of the

Copperheads were an all too common sight at the seminary. One was found basking on the floor under the radiator in the shower room.

Quite the eye opener early in the morning

fence. She stretched her neck over—nudged my chest and looked down at me with those big, brown eyes. Glancing away for a moment, I felt a gentle tug on my hand. Jane had the carrot! And, yes, my fingers were still all intact. We worked our way up to the house where Bert introduced us to his wife, Aggie. As we sat in their living room, I couldn't help but notice the sparse furnishings. These were folks of very modest means. Apart from a table and a few chairs, there were no pictures on the walls or decorations to speak of. Aggie offered to make us a cup of coffee. At first I was reluctant to accept, thinking that she should save it for herself and her husband. However, refusing would have been an insult. She served it in china cups and saucers and asked if we took cream or sugar. The coffee was a gesture out of respect to us as seminarians. To her we represented the clergy.

Bert and Aggie talked about their kids, the ups and downs of their marriage, and their struggles just to make ends meet. It seemed like an hour flew by in no time at all. We reluctantly had to say goodbye as other visits awaited us. As we drove away, I took one parting glance at Jane munching contently on grass in the pasture.

'Mark Hopkins' - vintage Reed & Barton® coffee pot -
San Francisco

North Beach

Apart from rekindling old friendships, Glen and I planned a weekend of coffee tasting and visiting cafés in the North Beach neighborhood. San Francisco was only a short commute from Walnut Creek on BART (Bay Area Rapid Transit). As we entered the Transbay Tube, the sunlight disappeared and interior lights popped on within seconds. The sound shifted from a high pitched hum to screeching or howling. Glen was quick to reassure me that being in the Tube, beneath the bay, was the safest place in the event of an earthquake. His words did not necessarily instill a vote of confidence. However, it wasn't long until we surfaced at the Embarcadero Station. Hopping on a cable car would get us closer to our first stop, Caffé Roma Coffee Roasting Company.

Once inside, our eyes were drawn to the bright red and gleaming brass Probat® roaster. The aroma was unmistakable—roasting coffee and brewed espresso. Glen ordered a latté. My choice was a doppio. I tried to impress the barista by ordering it in Italian. He just stood there with a puzzled look on his face. Finally, I just said, "I'll take a double espresso please." The coffee was served in classic chocolate brown cups. We sat down at the tables, flanked on both sides by stacks of coffee bags. It was

Enjoying a cup of coffee with my barista, Heather

reminiscent of a vintage 1950s malt shop—marble top tables and bent wood chairs. The gentle breeze swept through the café bringing a plethora of aromas. We enjoyed our coffee and took one last look at the Probat® on the way out.

Next stop, Tosca Café. Dating back to 1919, it has been a favorite haunt of many celebrities. As you walked through the vintage double doors, you were greeted by a very tall espresso machine on the corner of the bar. Lined up in a row were eight or ten bell-shaped glasses, each containing a teaspoon. "Those are for the cappuccinos," explained Glen. Interestingly, this cappuccino did not contain even an ounce of coffee. Instead, it was made with Ghiradelli® chocolate, steamed milk, and brandy—their way of disguising the booze during times of prohibition. It didn't take me long to discover why this drink was so popular. It warmed all the way down. I tapped into a little piece of Tosca history with every sip.

As the evening drew near, Glen wanted to take me to one of his favorite restaurants for dinner. This was not on the list of eateries well known to the casual tourist. Instead it was Scoma's, the place where the locals eat—not to mention many celebrities. We were quickly seated at what had to be one

"Retirement is one great big coffee break."

.....*Unknown author*

of the best tables in the place—commanding view of the setting sun, fisherman boats, and the wharf. Perusing the menu, I looked to Glen for advice on what to order. He suggested the sand dabs. The puzzled look on my face prompted him to say, "Trust me, you'll love them." He was right. They were absolutely delicious, especially covered in the almondine sauce. Glen's choice was the Petrale sole. Keep in mind that Scoma's prided themselves on freshness. The seafood on the menu was caught by their fleet on that very day.

A gentleman at the next table was ordering Cioppino (fish stew). This certainly brought back memories of a time when I prepared a bouillabaisse for a friend on Father's Day. Flying in fresh seafood to Fort Wayne for the special day was indeed challenging. However, the smile on Bill's face when he took his first bite made all of the preparation worthwhile.

Glen and I reminisced about the day—all of the cafés that we had visited and the wonderful coffee that we had sampled. A fitting end to our dinner would be some of Scoma's house coffee. They didn't disappoint. It was brewed to perfection. It is said that you can judge a good restaurant by the cof-

Jabez Burns & Sons sample roaster

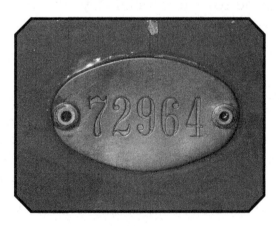

Jabez Burns ID plate

fee that it serves. That being said, Scoma's would be at the top of my list. The food, the coffee and the atmosphere certainly defined this as a *dolce far niente* moment. Regrettably, we had to call it a night and head back to Walnut Creek. The evening may have been drawing to a close but the coffee journey was just beginning.

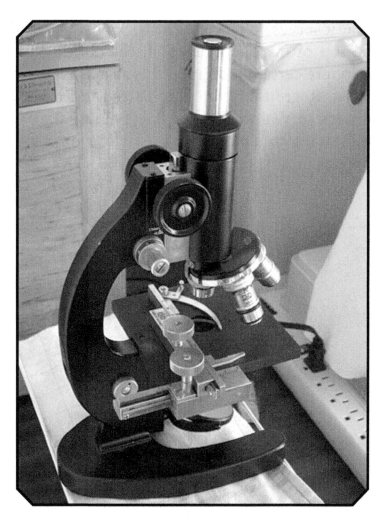

Beck & Sohne microscope with an incredible history

It's a Small World

Christmas Eve on the farm as a kid was nothing short of magical. The moonlight shimmering on the freshly fallen snow silhouetted the blue spruces and occasionally a rabbit or two. We always celebrated the blessed event by inviting family and friends over for dinner. Our front room, with the decorated tree in the corner, would soon be transformed into a dining room. My task was dragging out the leaves from the closet to make the table bigger. My sister would be entrusted with retrieving the china and silverware from the cherry hutch and setting the table. The menu for the evening would be beef stroganoff, freshly baked rolls, cranberry salad, and the list goes on. Pecan pie, raw apple cake, date pinwheel cookies, and various candies were dessert options along with freshly brewed coffee—always served with half & half. My grandmother actually made some of the best coffee. Ironically, she could never take a sip—as it would trigger an attack of vertigo.

We had a standing rule when it came to opening presents. As the clock struck 7:30pm, it was time to open my first gift under the tree. Gifts from Santa were opened on Christmas day. Carefully unwrapping the box, I couldn't believe me eyes. Oh my gosh, it was a microscope! I was just as excited as Ralphie in *A Christmas Story*, except that this wasn't

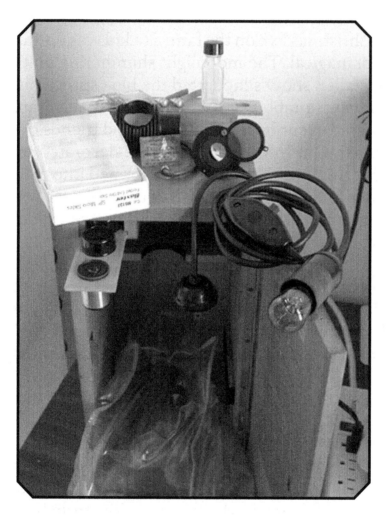

All for $20 - storage case, dust cover and accessories

a BB gun and there wasn't any risk of shooting my eye out. That little instrument, standing only six inches tall, opened up a whole new world of exploration—providing hours and hours of entertainment. Even though the gift was probably intended for my sister as well—I claimed it. Examining anything and everything, I would make sketches using our high tech tool of the day, colored pencils.

Years would pass and I would find myself sitting for some national board exams. In preparation, it was necessary to review my old pathology slides. However, I didn't have a microscope. An eBay search located one in Florida. It was an old German scope (Beck & Sohne) and seemed to have all the bells and whistles not to mention the very attractive price of only $20. How could I go wrong? It arrived in its original oak storage case. Among the accessories inside was a special glass slide that was used for manually counting red and white blood cells (hemocytometer). I recognized it from my training days as a hospital corpsman in the Navy. It alone was worth more than the microscope and the accesories put together. More significantly, it gave me a clue as to the original owner—my hunch, laboratory technologist or medical student? The dust cover was very yellowed and extremely brittle. I handled it with kid loves as it was very difficult to unfold without

When describing a medical condition, I was asked, "Can't you find any longer word than that?" As a matter of fact I said "yes —

pneumonoultramicroscopic silicovolcanoconiosis."

I am sure that another word, perhaps longer that this one, will emerge somewhere down the road. However, I am content, at least for now, in having met my friend's challenge.

cracking. Sewn into the seam was a label with the handwritten name of the owner (initials C.T.) and where they had attended medical school. Searching online, I was able to find a graduation yearbook including his picture. C.T. went on to become a surgeon, military officer and educator. Eventually moving to Seattle he assumed the duties as section chief at a well known medical clinic. Amazingly, a former classmate of mine, now a retired priest, had worked with him at that very clinic. They were colleagues— what a coincidence!

I often wondered what happened to C.T.— did he retire, what was his career like over the years? Then quite by accident I found his memorial in a military publication. It answered not only those questions but provided a rather lengthy list of his many accolades. I think that he would be pleased to know that his microscope fell into good hands— beginning its journey with him and continuing its journey with me.

"Any customer can have a car painted any color he wants so long as it is black."

....Henry Ford, regarding the Model T

Happy Days

School was out and summer was just around the corner. My cousin Walter or as I called him, W. K. offered me a job of helping him around his small family farm.

He had retired as an inspector for the U. S. Dept. of Agriculture - Bureau of Chemistry. Formally trained in botany, he held both a Bachelor's and Master's degree from Michigan Agricultural College. The farm was not only home to him as a boy, but now a place to relax and enjoy his retirement.

Apart from cutting the grass, each day would be filled with a new adventure. Once such day included hand cranking, starting and driving a Model T. He warned me, "Be careful, that crank can snap back and hit your arm." It took several turns to 'advance the spark.' But then on the last try, it started up and purred like a kitten. I didn't get hurt but my arm felt like it was about ready to fall off. Any pain or agony was soon replaced by the thrill of driving around the property. The old Model T had more pick up than I had ever imagined. I was driving way too fast, but W. K. never said a word. He just smiled.

Everything was a buzz when we approached the bee hives. From a bee's perspective, this was paradise. Why, because just a few yards away was

W. K. on the farm picking apples
September 30, 1980 - Age 91

an orchard with row after row of apple trees in full blossom. They could fly over, get their fill of nectar, and be back in the hive in no time at all. W. K. helped me don my bee keeping suit and attach the tie-down veil that covered my head and face. Our plan was to smoke the hives and remove the honey, hopefully without getting stung. The smoke worked like a charm. The bees were very content as long as you were gentle and moved slowly. We took the harvested honey back to the house and worked in the basement where it was nice and cool. Most of the honey was spun down in a big centrifuge, separating it from the comb. The rest of it was cut into sections and put into jars. That was my favorite way to enjoy it—comb and all.

Lunchtime at the farm was always exciting when we fired up the old wood burning stove. Compared to cooking on grandma's electric range, this was definitely an involved process—putting in the kindling, adjusting the draft, turning this knob, pulling that lever. The hamburgers were already beginning to sizzle in the cast iron skillet. We sopped up the leftover drippings with the buns—definitely not a heart healthy choice, but oh so good! I drew some water to make the coffee. It wasn't just a simple matter of turning on the tap. You had to

French enameled Biggin pot - 1865

prime the pitcher pump at the sink. I pumped and pumped and pumped. Finally water came gushing out. It wasn't long until the coffee was ready. But there wasn't any cream! Being a 'man,' I decided to drink it black. W.K. said, "That will put hair on your chest!" Little did we know at the time, I would need more hair on my head than on my chest.

W.K.'s farm house was chock-full of antiques—many of them still in working order. I cranked up the Victrola in the corner and listened to the music. It was hard to believe that such a loud, clear and beautiful sound was coming out of a machine that used *no electricity*. And then there were the books—many dating back to the time of Lincoln. Although W. K. encouraged me to browse, I was afraid to even even open the covers. Hanging on a wall was a beautiful regulator clock . It filled the entire room with its soothing tick tocks and mellow chimes. My eye was drawn to an office model Remington® typewriter sitting on the roll top desk. When asked about it W. K. was quick to offer one of his many pearls of wisdom. He said, "If you can type, you will always have a good job." Taking his advice to heart, I en-

Victorian trade card (Front)
packed inside a bag of Lion Coffee

rolled in a typing class that next summer at my local high school. It was a little awkward being the only boy in the class. However, it was all worth it when I got back my first typewritten paper with a big 'A' at the top. Typing also spared me from many bad duty assignments in the Navy not to mention helping me through college.

To say that W. K. had a green thumb was an understatement. His truck patch was a page right out of *Crockett's Victory Garden* (WGBH, Boston). He had the uncanny expertise of knowing exactly when to pick the fruit and vegetables—at the peak of their flavor. He didn't keep his bounty for himself but shared it with family and friends. He was always a welcomed sight whenever he drove up in the Olds Ninety-Eight. Out came the wicker basket full of fresh produce—peaches, tomatoes, sweet corn and the list goes on.

When it was time for W.K. to finally let go of the farm, he invited me to choose any of the books in the study. It was a hard decision. After perusing the shelves for awhile, I found a volume that had once drawn my attention as a boy. It was the first edition (1865) of *Life of Abraham Lincoln* by Joseph H. Barrett, the noted biographer and historian. The spine was finished in hand-tooled leather with the

CHILDREN'S
DOLLS WITH
STORIES.

SERIES OF 30 KINDS.

One in each package of

LION COFFEE.

YANKEE DOODLE.

Yankee Doodle came to town,
Riding on a pony,
He stuck a feather in his cap,
And called it macaroni.—Ref.

And there was Captain Washington,
Upon a slapping stallion,
And giving orders to his men,
I guess there was a million.—Ref.

And then the feathers on his hat,
They looked so tarnal finey,
I wanted peskily to get,
To give to my Jemima.—Ref.

Once Johnny Bull lived in New York
But he has moved away, sir,
For Yankee Doodle came along,
And said he must not stay, sir.

REFRAIN.
Yankee Doodle, ha, ha, ha, Cakes and sugar candy,
Come listen to the story now of Yankee Doodle Dandy.

Lion Coffee

THE GREAT TEMPERANCE DRINK.

Bend back the lower end of this doll, so it will stand up.

Victorian trade card (Back)

edges printed in a colorful, marbelized pattern—a sign of quality book binding back in the day. Just inside, under a piece of vellum was a wonderful lithograph of Lincoln.

W. K. left the study and returned shortly thereafter with a gift in hand. He said, "I think this will bring back some memories." It was *The ABC and XYZ of Bee Culture (1910)* by A. I. Root. Considered to be the 'bible of beekeeping'—it was his source to maintaining hives and harvesting honey. Now, it was being entrusted to me with the hope of passing it on to future generations.

W. K. lived well into his nineties. In fact he was picking apples on his ninety-first birthday. It was indeed an honor and a privilege to spend the summers with him. Much of what I use in my everyday life I learned from him. What an incredible man!

Pot from the Welsh Produce Café -
High Street, Swansea, South Wales

A Long Way from Home

It was almost twenty-two years ago when a small, oval-shaped coffee pot caught my eye in the gift shop of a department store in Portland, Oregon. Catering to ladies' fashions and mens' clothing, this well known store also featured live piano music and a café. The gift shop had a variety of one-of-a-kind, unusual gifts—everything from Waterford® and Baccarat® crystal to delectable chocolates. This particular coffee pot had the inscription, 'Welsh Produce Café.' The attached tag explained that it was part of a collection of vintage hotelware from England. Restored to a gleaming luster it was absolutely stunning. I just could not resist—purchase price: $65. It found a good home in my china cabinet along with other treasures. Over the years, tarnishing would take its toll—turning it almost black. Then, a resurrection of sorts took place. I decided to get to the bottom of its origins. Always in the back of my mind was the lingering question of what or where was the Welsh Produce Café. By the silver marks on the bottom, I knew that the pot had been produced by Walker and Hall of Sheffield in the early 1930s. Where it was used and put into service remained a mystery. Following a hunch, I contacted several lo-

A "social" will be held in connection with the Wounded Soldiers' Side-car Outing Club at the Welsh Produce Cafe. High-street, Swansea, on Thursday next, when about 30 wounded ,ldiers .'1 be in attendance. Mr. Thom s, t.he proprietor, is providing t e s.l lie:s with teas. The "social" will commence at 2 50, and tea will be served it 30. S .me excellent singers will contribute towards the musical programme, ar d dur'ng tl e afternoon the men will hav? pl nry of games to amuse themselves with.

Newspaper clipping honoring wounded soldiers at the Welsh Produce Café, "Cambria Daily Leader" - (November 18, 1916)

cal Welsh societies, a national museum in Wales, and an auction house in Cardiff. Among the three, someone might be able to shed some light. About three weeks later I got a call from one of the society's members in Seattle. She had found an article in the *Cambria Daily Leader* (A daily English language newspaper, circulated in South and West Wales) dated November 18, 1916. Apparently, the proprietor of the **Welsh Produce Café** was holding a "social" for wounded soldiers at his establishment on High Street in Swansea. This was incredible news! This was the first step in establishing a provenance. Even though my coffee pot was produced fourteen or so years later, it was conceivable that it came from that very café in Swansea—all evidence pointing in that direction.

However, my mood quickly turned from one of excitement to somberness, realizing that the Swansea Battallion suffered huge casualties at the Battle of Mametz Wood in Northern France—just a few months before the article was written. Robert Graves, a poet, who actually fought in the battle, described the scene in vivid detail (p. 106).

Battle of Mametz Wood
July 7, 1916

"It was full of dead Prussian Guards, big men and dead Royal Fusiliers and South Wales Borderers, little men. Not a single tree in the wood remained unbroken."

....Robert Graves, poet

On the home front, my grandfather, a First Sergeant in the U.S. Army infantry, also found himself immersed in the trenches, as the U.S. entered the war in April of 1917. As a kid, I would dress up and play soldier, wearing his 'doughboy' helmet—unaware of its true significance as a piece of his battle gear. Grandpa never talked about the war with me at least. Being only six or seven, he was definitely sparing me from such atrocities. He came back from the Army, safe and sound. Others were not so lucky.

It's so intriguing to think that a little coffee pot, steeped in so much world history, would find it's way some 4,800 miles to Portland and end up as part of my collection. Imagine all the stories it could tell if only it could talk.

*Connie enjoying a cup of coffee at breakfast
in the Park Blocks - Portland, 1992*

Recipes

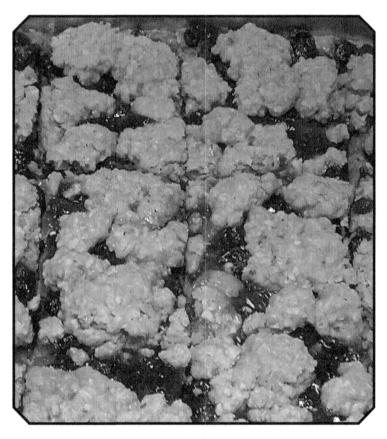

T & J's Oatmeal Raisin Bars -
soft and chewy

Oatmeal Raisin Bars

Cream Together
1/2 cup butter (half butter, half margarine)
2/3 cup brown sugar (packed)
1 egg, beaten
1/2 teaspoon vanilla

Add Dry Ingredients
1 cup all-purpose four
1 cup quick-cooking oatmeal
1/4 teaspoon baking soda
1/4 teaspoon cinnamon

Cook Filling
Low heat in medium saucepan until thick
and bubbly.

1/2 cup water
1 cup raisins
2 teaspoons cornstarch mixed with 3 tablespoons white sugar

1. Preheat oven to 325°. Bake for 30 min. until lightly brown. Cool.

2. Spread half of dough mixture in 9 x 9 ungreased square pan. Spread filling mixture on top of dough. Crumble remaining dough mixture on top of filling.

Glaze (Optional)
1. 2 tablespoons butter, 1 1/2 c. powdered sugar, 1/2 teaspoon vanilla, drop of almond extract, milk-to make drizzle consistency. Drizzle over the top.

Molly's Buttermilk Sugar Cookies -
right out of the oven

Buttermilk Sugar Cookies
(Yields 4 or 5 dozen)

Cream Together

1 1/2 cup granulated sugar

1 cup shortening or 2 sticks butter

2 eggs, beaten

Add To Mixture

4 cups all-purpose flour

1 tablespoon baking soda (level)

1 teaspoon baking powder (heaping)

1/8 teaspoon almond extract

1 tablespoon vanilla

1 cup buttermilk (add alternately with flour)

1. Chill dough.

2. Roll out 1/2 inch thick and cut with cookie cutter.

3. Bake on greased cookie sheet, 325° for 30 minutes. Dust with flour.

Biscotti
biscuit

...a tradition with coffee, this hard cookie is twice-baked, great for just dunking or gift giving

Almond Biscotti
(Yields 48)

Combine
1/2 cup butter (room temperature)
3 eggs, beaten
1 cup sugar

Add To Mixture
2 1/2 cups all-purpose flour
1 teaspoon baking powder
1 1/2 cups slivered almonds, toasted

1. Knead the dough on a lightly floured board for a couple of minutes. Cut the dough in half, forming two loaves, each about 2 inches in diameter. Put the loaves on a greased baking sheet.

3. Bake for 25 minutes at 350° or until slightly browned.

4. Cut into slices about 1/2 inch thick. Place on their sides continuing to bake at 350° for another 10 minutes.

Old Fashioned Sugar Cream Pie -
rich and creamy

Old Fashioned Sugar Cream Pie

1 1/2 cups sugar
1/3 cup all-purpose flour
1/2 teaspoon salt
2 1/2 cups heavy whipping cream
2 teaspoons pure vanilla extract
1 tablespoon melted butter

1. Blend sugar, flour, salt. Stir in cream, vanilla extract, butter. Thoroughly beat and pour into pie crust. I used a Pillsbury® ready-made crust.

2. Bake 10 min. at 400°, 25 min. at 325°.

3. Serve slightly warm. Dust with cinnamon.

PS: Our family always said that Maggie Barnes, my cousin's grandmother, made the best sugar cream pies. Her secret: stirring the ingredients together in the pie shell with her forefinger—a tradition which we have carried on to this day.

Snickerdoodles

...a simple cookie,
yet a surprisingly elegant
accompaniment to coffee

Snickerdoodles
(Yields 36)

1/2 cup unsalted butter (room temperature}
1 cup sugar
1/4 teaspoon baking soda
1/4 teaspoon cream of tartar
1 egg
1/2 teaspoon pure vanilla extract
1 1/2 cups all-purpose flour
2 teaspoons sugar
1 teaspoon ground cinnamon

1. In a bowl beat the butter with an electric mixer or wire whisk until creamy. Add 1 cup sugar, cream of tartar and baking soda. Beat until combined. Beat in 1 egg and vanilla extract until combined. Beat in as much flour as you can. Add the rest with a spoon or spatula. Chill 30 minutes.

2. In a bowl combine 2 tablespoons sugar with cinnamon. Form dough into 1" balls and roll in cinnamon/sugar mixture.

3. Bake 2 inches apart, 375° for 10-11 minutes.

Pumpkin cupcakes - incredibly delicious and moist.
Recipe on facing page yields about 15 medium-sized
cupcakes.

Pumpkin Bread
from Jane Vogland
(Makes one 5 x 8 pan)

1-1/2 cups granulated sugar
1 cup pumpkin puree
1/2 cup canola oil
1/4 cup water
2 large eggs

1-3/4 cups all-purpose flour
1 teaspoon baking soda
1 teaspoon salt
1/2 teaspoon cinnamon
1/2 teaspoon nutmeg

In a large mixing bowl, mix liquid ingredients (sugar through eggs) together with beaters or a whisk. In another bowl mix dry ingredients (flour through nutmeg). Fold dry ingredients into wet. Do not over mix. Pour into oiled bread pan. Bake at 325° for 40 minutes and test. If knife comes out clean, it's ready. If soft in center, bake a few more minutes. May add chopped pecans or walnuts to batter. Set pan on cake rack for five minutes. Turn out onto cake rack to cool. Enjoy!

Photo and Illustration Credits

My sister, myself and Buttons, p. 6 - Author
Mirro-Matic, p. 8 - Author
Hospitality snack plate, p. 10 - Author
Hills Bros, can, p. 12 - Author
Hills Bros. scoop, p. 12 - Author
Kaldi and the goats, p. 14 - *All About Coffee,*
    William H. Ukers
Maxwell House Coffee ad., p. 18,
    Good Housekeeping, Nov. 1926
Caffeine symbol, p. 22 - Author
Monarch coffee jar, p. 24 - Author
Lion Coffee Line card (Front), p. 26 - Author
Lion Coffee Line card (Back), p. 26 - Author
Golden West coffee jar, p. 28 - Author
Increase Wilson grinder, p. 30 - Author
Increase Wilson plate, p. 31 - Author
In The Warehouse, p. 34 - Brandy Rowell
Julian Public Library, p. 36 - Author
Anza-Borrego, landscape, p. 38 - Author
Roger and Glen preparing food, p. 38 - Author
"I can still taste those steaks", p. 40 - Author
At the summit, p. 42 - Author
Arrowhead found at Anza-Borrego, p. 42 - Author
Pulling the roast, p. 44 - Brandy Rowell
"The Coffee Break", p. 48 - Author

Photo and Illustration Credits

Jamaica Blue Mtn. coffee barrel, p. 50 - Author
Coffee tin, p. 52 - Author
Cafetiere or French press, p. 54 - Wendell Henry
The Drake teaspoon, p. 58 - Author
Lou Mitchell's (top), p. 64 - Used By Permission
Lou Mitchell's (bottom) p. 64 - Used By Permission
Lou Mitchell's p. 66 - Used By Permission
The Academy bell tower, p. 68 - Author
Copy of "All About Coffee", p. 72 - Author
Mark Hopkins pot, p. 78 - Author
Enjoying a cup of coffee, p. 80 - Derya Ruggles
Jabez Burns roaster, p. 84 - Brandy Rowell
Jabez Burns ID plate, p. 84 - Brandy Rowell
Beck & Sohne microscope, p. 86 - Author
All For $20 dust cover, p. 88 - Author
W. K. on the farm, p. 94 - Author
French enameled Biggin pot, p. 96 - Author
Victorian trade card (Front), p. 98 - Author
Victorian trade card (Back), p. 100 - Author
Welsh Produce Café pot, p. 102 - Author
Newspaper clipping p. 104 - *Cambria Daily Leader*
Connie, p. 108 - Used by permission
T & J's Oatmeal Raisin Bars, p. 110 - Author
Mollie's Buttermilk Sugar Cookies, p. 112 - Author
Old Fashioned Sugar Cream Pie, p. 116 - Author

Photo and Illustration Credits

Pumpkin Cupcakes, p. 120 - Author
Back To Work, p. 127 - Author

Cowgirl and Golden West® Coffee Can, Title page - Closset & Devers, 1931

Sources

• *All About Coffee,* William H. Ukers, The Tea and Coffee Trade Journal Company, Second Edition, 1935.
• *Coffee*, Jill Norman, New York, Bantam Books, 1992.
• *Coffee Basics*, Kevin Knox & Julie Sheldon Huffaker, New York, John Wiley & Sons, 1997.
• *Coffee The Essential Guide To The Essential Bean*, Catherine Calvert, New York, Hearst Books, 1994.
• *Crockett's Victory Garden,* Produced by WGBH in Boston & Dist. by PBS.
• *Espresso Coffee*, Andreas Illy & Rinantonio Viani, San Diego, Academic Press, 1995.
• *Espresso - Culture And Cuisine*, Karl Petzke & Sara Slavin, San Francisco, Chronicle Books, 1994.
• *Starbucks Passion For Coffee*, Starbucks Corporation, Sunset Publishing, 1994.
• *The Book Of Coffee*, Francesco & Ricardo Illy, New York, Abbeyville press, 1989.
• *Uncommon Grounds*, Mark Pendergrast, New York, Basic Books, 1999.

Disclaimer

I have tried to recreate events, locales and conversations from my memories of them. In order to maintain their anonymity in some instances, I have changed the names of individuals and places. Although I have made every effort to ensure that the information in this book is accurate, I do not claim to be an expert and hereby disclaim any liability to any party.

Coffee Break Is Over

In the bottom of the cup (as illustrated on page 48) you would see this when finishing your coffee.

The coffee break may be over but my writing continues. Look for more *Peaberry Chronicles* to follow.

"Ti auguro molte buone tazze di caffè"
(I wish you many good cups of coffee).

M. G. M.

Notes

Notes

About the Author

When other kids snickered at the thought of coffee, this Pacific Northwest author embraced it—grabbing every sip he could get.

His careers and educational pursuits have taken him all over the country—providing the foundation for many personal stories. With a unique perspective, diverse background and attention to detail, he lends a high degree of authenticity and credibility to his writing—drawing the reader into the stories as if they were there themselves.

Made in the USA
Middletown, DE
15 August 2021